# Praise for JAM

## THE
# JOURNEYMAN'S
### GUIDE

"Over the course of my 23 year career as an agent, I have negotiated over 500 contracts for professional basketball players in the NBA, NBDL and the Overseas Leagues. I believe *The Journeyman's Guide* is a valuable tool for any player who aspires to start a career in professional basketball. Although a player can never be completely prepared for the myriad of problems that may arise, this Guide gives a thorough overview of the business side of professional basketball. As an agent, one of my jobs is to educate players about the very process that the authors of *The Journeyman's Guide* break down in this publication. The current and former players who provide testimonials all provide valuable insight that can give the aspiring young ballplayer the knowledge necessary to navigate the extremely competitive and challenging business of professional basketball. This Guide should be required reading for players who are near the end of their collegiate basketball careers"

—Andrew Vye, *ASM Sports*

"James and Ronnie are two of the most professional student athletes I've ever coached. Their approach to the game of basketball was very polished. Not only did they perform and become All-League performers on the basketball court, they excelled in the classroom and in the community. I am not surprised by the extensive careers that the both of them have had. James and Ronnie have ten plus years of international playing experience. That experience equates to an abundance of first hand knowledge in dealing with agents and international play. *The Journeyman's Guide* is 100% real and authentic from two great players that have lived it."

—Fran McCaffery, *Iowa Hawkeyes*

"I have trained NBA and overseas players, consulted with international teams, been a part of some groundbreaking projects for the NBA, and even played overseas for 7 years. One thing remains true, the journey of playing overseas is often challenging to explain. Every country, league, and team is different, and players can have multiple perspectives on what we classify as the same process. With that said, *The Journeyman's Guide* does an amazing job pulling together the commonalities, highlighting and detailing the experience, and educating the next wave of players. Without a doubt, this will serve as a terrific resource for any player preparing to play overseas!"

—Jeremiah Boswell, *NBA Consultant*

"*The Journeyman's Guide* is a must read for any aspiring professional basketball player looking to get insight into what to expect playing basketball overseas or in the D-League. The topics covered will help players understand what it takes to make it, as well as answer many questions players may have as they begin their professional career abroad. An incredibly valuable resource!"

—Bryan Bailey, *Westchester Knicks*

"In over 46 years of experience, our company established itself as the European leader in sports marketing, helping thousands of players to sign with the right team. As a manager, I know how finding a team or signing a contract is not enough. It's our duty to help the player find the perfect job opportunities in order for him to grow and develop into an all-around pro player. That means being ready to hop on a plane and bounce to a foreign country just to prove his skills and build his numbers. Players have to understand that signing overseas is not the failure of the NBA dream, but a great opportunity to work on themselves and hopefully reach that dream. And that's how *The Journeyman's Guide* comes into play. This book is a collection of the know-how from players, coaches and managers with plenty of international experience. It's a state of mind that every player who wants to go pro needs to achieve before jumping into the European challenge. Definitely the perfect reading for all college students that want to start their professional basketball career."

—Manuel Capicchioni, *Interperformances*

"A great manual - guidebook for all players and their families. It would make the perfect farewell graduation gift from colleges to senior players. Something like a 'fellowship of knowledge' for the new professional basketball life overseas!"

—Nikos Varlas, *Eurohoops.net*

# THE JOURNEYMAN'S GUIDE

## FACILITATE YOUR HOOP JOURNEY OVERSEAS!
### THE INS AND OUTS TO SUCCESS.

## JAMES MAYE AND RONALD BURRELL

Published by MHJ Books

Paperback ISBN: 978-0-692-81181-8

First Edition First Printing, February 2017

Printed in the United States of America

*We thank God first for blessing us, as well as our families whom have always been the foundation of our support. We also would like to thank all the players who have contributed by sharing their testimonies in the guide. And last, but not least, we show gratitude to all the coaches, players, and members of the basketball community that we ran into along the way that aided us in realizing the necessity of such a guide and it ultimately coming to fruition.*

# CONTENTS

# THE JOURNEYMAN'S GUIDE

# DO YOU WANT TO BE A JOURNEYMAN?

With almost no long-term contracts, various styles of play, and a wide range of living and travel conditions, the professional life of an international player can present many challenges. Don't forget to add a dose of foreign culture to that mix. Basketball players who don't end up having a long term NBA career often bounce around from team to team or country to country. These globetrotters we label JOURNEYMEN can make a good living and have a career full of priceless experiences. With games played in 43 different countries while being members of teams from 16 of them, the two co-authors of this guide encompass to full extent the meaning of the term, having a combined journey that spans nearly every continent, market and level of basketball "overseas". After advising so many along our paths and seeing numerous young players ruin potentially lucrative careers due to being ill prepared to endure the rigors of this line of work, this book is a tool to educate and enlighten. Spoken words often go misinterpreted, unabsorbed or forgotten. From the eyes of the athletes who live it, in written form, we present this guide full of information to better prepare you to positively experience a professional basketball career overseas!

To the casual American fan, the NBA is the only professional basketball that matters. However, within the last two decades, the game has globalized, minor leagues have become more prevalent, and basketball as a whole has become one of the most popular sports in the world, second only to soccer. Professional basketball jobs are measured by the thousands worldwide for Americans alone. In the NBA, on opening night of the 2016-2017 season, 436. With the NBA rosters featuring a record 113 international players, only 323 of those NBA players were American. Let's assume that 2/3's of those jobs were guaranteed, multi-year deals. That leaves you with about 215 American players with rock solid NBA contracts. All other professional players will be considered journeymen at some point in their careers, encountering various options to live their "dream" life on the hardwood.

Here's the bottom line! The basketball world is large and expanding. The majority of professional basketball players will not have a smooth, linear career with the same support system throughout, like many of the NBA players we watch daily. Many will be faced with tough challenges thousands of miles from their comfort zones. These adversities create some of the most compelling and unique stories in sports that widely go untold... and some possibly avoidable situations. Along with talent and hard work, building a successful career in the global basketball market takes knowledge and savvy, some of which can be imparted by those who have already navigated those faraway and unsteady waters. From breaking down the agent hiring process to culture adjustment, from preseason preparation to money management and everything in between, this informative guide gives you everything necessary to put a prosperous, yet seemingly distant, professional career within your grasp. Without further ado, let's become a pro!

# BECOMING A PRO

# GETTING STARTED

After a successful collegiate career, any athlete with hopes of becoming a pro is faced with finding an agent.

For the lucky ones, you will have the choice of a number of agents who have done their homework and are interested in you. This interest normally comes in the mail or by phone to your home or to your college coach. This makes the process easier in that all you will have to do is choose. But do so wisely. Discern the good agents from the bad by using a couple of tools. First, do your homework. Know as much, if not more about them as they do about you. With the help of your college coach or a mentor, examine the agent's resume, clientele and reputation. If you like what you see, ask him what his vision is for your career and get a feel for how high he may think your ceiling is. Be sure to ask what short-term steps he plans to take that will propel you to your long-term goals. Not having those ideas in mind is the sign of a poorly prepared agent and likely not your best choice.

You want an agent with the same confidence in your game as you have, but try to be realistic. Be comfortable that the agent knows you well. Otherwise, he will not put you in the best situation. Depending on your goals, choose an agent who fits your needs. If you are an NBA prospect, hire an agent with NBA clients. See what they have done with players that have playing styles and resumes

We Are Basketball

*These FIBA registered trademarks are used for illustration purposes and with the authorization of FIBA. FIBA cannot be associated with the content published in this book.*

5

comparable to yours. If you are looking to play overseas, make sure your agent has the right connections and is FIBA-certified.

FIBA is the governing body of basketball and regulates the activity of players' agents. Agents often specialize in specific regions so know where their expertise lies. Are they strong in countries where players like you are proven to be successful? Lastly, how many clients does this agent have? Too few... perhaps not enough experience. Too many... perhaps not enough time to dedicate to you individually. Dealing with agents is tricky. Always remember an agent works for you, not the other way around. They need you to make money and you need an agent to get your career off the ground. But the player is the talent and the money machine. You've got the leverage. A good agent communicates well and often. The first sign of a bad agent is one that doesn't answer phone calls and emails. Keep these points in mind and go with your gut. You can always change agents at any time in your career, usually with a simple letter and two-week notice. Be careful to do so in a cordial manner, as not to burn bridges. It's a business decision and never personal. You never know when you may need to revert back to them during the latter part of your career.

> Dealing with agents is tricky. At the end of the day, remember an agent works for you, not the other way around.

For those who may not have a ton of agents knocking down your door, the process is different. This could be because you played at a smaller school or were buried in the shadow of a teammate at a big time program. All the same, you lacked exposure. So, it's important to be proactive. This means attending workouts, camps, and invitationals. It means sending your own film, emails and phone inquiries. Don't be afraid to pay for entry into an exposure camp or ask for someone to loan you the money to do so. Invest in yourself and your career! You will be able to repay them promptly should you perform well. Just as mentioned earlier in this section, do your homework. Research thoroughly before choosing any camps and invitationals. Some will just be attempts to make money for the directors with very few pro agents, scouts or teams present. Find the ones who are legit.

Whatever you have to do to get an agent that believes you can be a pro and wants to sign you, you've got to do. Cash in on favors and don't be afraid to ask for help. Other teammates and coaches will have connections, let them know of your interest and see if they can help get you in front of an agent looking for prospects. Without opportunity, there is no success.

Remember, don't fill your plate with more than you can handle. In other words, an agent is an investment. You want him to take the same level of risks that you are willing to take, to represent the same risk-reward factor as you. Some agents are aggressive, always pushing your potential earnings to the limit. They turn down deals left and right looking for something better. This may mean you are not on the first wave of flights overseas which leave in August. It may be a waiting game! If you can't stomach sitting at home for a couple of extra weeks or months, while your friends are over the waters gearing up for preseason action, this may not be the right agent for you. On the other hand, some agents are passive. They are always willing to sign you to the first semi-decent contract offer that comes across their desk. The good thing with these agents is that you almost always have a job. Sometimes, in the long term, not all of these jobs will be in your best interest as a player, leaving you feeling unchallenged and undervalued. No matter which you choose, you are the captain of this ship so make sure most, if not all, of your individual desires as a player are met and fulfilled.

> Whatever you have to do to get an agent that believes you can be a pro and wants to sign you, you've got to do.

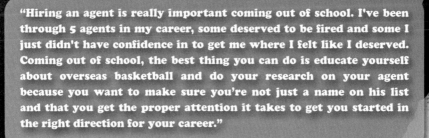

*Ricky Hickman, PG/SG (UNCG '07)*
*Passport: USA/Georgia*
*Pro Career: Italy, Germany, Turkey*
*2014 Euroleague Champion*
*All-Euroleague Team*
*2016 Turkish Cup Champion*

"Hiring an agent is really important coming out of school. I've been through 5 agents in my career, some deserved to be fired and some I just didn't have confidence in to get me where I felt like I deserved. Coming out of school, the best thing you can do is educate yourself about overseas basketball and do your research on your agent because you want to make sure you're not just a name on his list and that you get the proper attention it takes to get you started in the right direction for your career."

# NOTES

TIP: It's good to jot down a few thoughts before meeting with any agent. Be sure that your
individual needs and expectations can be met.

_____

_____

_____

_____

_____

_____

_____

_____

_____

_____

_____

*__Don't forget to chronicle your journey with us at myhoopjourney.com__*

# CHASING THE NBA DREAM

Any player who doesn't have the dream of being an NBA player is selling himself short. After all, that's what the hard work, injuries, successes and failures have been about up to this point. The NBA is just about finding the right situation for many pro players. Timing is the key, unless of course you are just an overwhelming and rare talent, in which case you most likely have no use for this information.

With the emergence of the NBA Development league in 2001, many players have stayed stateside to be 'closer' to the NBA. As of 2016, there were 22 D-league teams who were all closely watched by their respective NBA affiliates. However, with the globalization of the game and scouting technology such as Synergy, no league goes unnoticed by NBA scouts. Although about 40% of current NBA players have spent time in the D-league, do not feel out of the running for an NBA shot if you play overseas! Perhaps you will miss the opportunity for an immediate call up, but those are few and far between. More often than not, a full season of international basketball has always

been more lucrative than a year in the D-league. As of the 2016-17 season, the D-league top salary earners, not attached to an NBA contract, made about $26,000 for the entire season. Those were the "A" players. "B" players made roughly $19,500.

**The NBA Gatorade League.** The D-league will be no more come the 2017-18 season. After a multiyear expanded partnership between the NBA and Gatorade, the league will be officially rebranded the NBA G-league. With that comes the Gatorade Sports Science Institute, which means innovative equipment and further enhancements in player sports performance and

Sioux Falls Skyforce
*Heat*

Reno Bighorns
*Kings*

Santa Cruz Warriors
*Warriors*

Salt Lake City Stars
*Jazz*

Oklahoma City Blue
*Thunder*

Los Angeles Defenders
*Lakers*

Austin Spurs
*Spurs*

Northern Arizona Suns
*Suns*

Texas Legends
*Mavericks*

Rio Grand Valley Vipers
*Rockets*

Grand Rapids Drive
*Pistons*

Iowa Energy
*Grizzles*

Windy City Bulls
*Bulls*

Canton Charge
*Cavaliers*

Erie Bayhawks
*Magic*

Fort Wayne Mad Ants
*Pacers*

Raptors 905
*Raptors*

Maine Red Claws
*Celtics*

Westchester Knicks
*Knicks*

Long Island Nets
*Nets*

Delaware 87ers
*76ers*

Greensboro Swarm
*Hornets*

recovery. With the potential improvements you can make as a player along with the steady increase in the number of teams each season, your chances to make the NBA have never been better. On top of that, there are new collective bargaining agreements in place and higher, more life-sustaining salaries rumored to be proposed for future seasons.

Depending on your individual situation, a G-league salary may not be substantially more money compared to other contract offers you may possibly have. However, it will be enough of a salary for a player coming from college who hasn't made a dime yet. Most aforementioned call-ups are actually NBA-contracted players that were temporarily sent down to their allocated teams and then brought back up. Simply watching the numbers shouldn't make you feel that you have a good chance at a 10-day contract. The odds are stacked against you. Many things have to be aligned for you to be one of the lucky few. You need a solid spot on the team, decent minutes and high production. Also, an NBA team must have a "need" for a player like you and it's essential that you be on the top of that list. Even then, it may still not be enough.

The G-league does not have to be skipped in order to be eligible to play overseas. If you are performing well, it can be used as a springboard to a decent pay bracket in international play for not only future seasons, but for the current one.

An overseas team can sign you out of the G-league at a hefty buyout price. For most international teams, this is an extremely high fee for a player unless you are performing at a high level. If you are, then you are probably on an NBA watch list anyway. In this situation, you may want to go ahead and stick the minor league season out. Your agent should have a feel of what your potential value is in the call-up market.

Whether the new name or its former, one thing you must know upon entering the G-league is that it is a full out grind. You are not in it for the pay. If making the NBA is your ultimate dream, you can't be. You are in it for the exposure. Everyone is! The players, coaches, video coordinators, referees, equipment managers, team executives, water boys and even the mascots are all subject for call-up review. So don't be surprised if people are willing to step on you to get your spotlight, bettering their chance at reaching the big stage of the NBA.

Most G-league coaches have strong connections in the NBA and abroad which can be vital to what the next step will be in your career. Stay sharp and be smart about the relationships you build within the chase. As one person moves up, if you are highly recommendable, there may be an open door for you as well in the near future.

If you decide to play in the G-league, it does not have to be in your first year out of college. NBA talent evaluators know your strengths and weaknesses. Sometimes it's better to head overseas to polish your game for a year or two before displaying yourself on that big stage. It will give scouts a chance to see your improvement which may help you get in the door. There will be a free flow of players from the G-league to overseas, overseas to G-league and from overseas to the NBA. What's most important is what you do on the hardwood, no matter where you play. If you have NBA level talent it will get noticed.

> The G-league is a full out grind. You are not in it for the pay. You are in it for the exposure.

Maurice Baker, PG (Oklahoma State '02)
Passport: USA
Pro Career: Russia, Lithuania, France, Philippines, Syria,
Puerto Rico, Dominican Republic, Mexico, Venezuela
Spent parts of 12 seasons in the D-League

"Just like the D-league, the G-league is a sacrifice! You may not make a lot of money but you will play in front of NBA scouts and general managers every night. The biggest error guys make is coming in thinking that they will be competing against mediocre talent. That's not true! Every night you will be facing guys that played for big time college basketball programs that may or may not have been drafted and are very close to getting called up to the NBA. You have to be ready. I won the championship my first year back when the D- league was one game per playoff round. The competition made it tough because guys were trying to get theirs. One bad night and you were going home. Now, as playoff series are the best of 3, you have more of a chance to bounce back after a bad game. One of the hardest parts for everybody is when your team's NBA affiliate assigns a player to the team. It can be even more difficult for the coach, as he has no control as the NBA team tells him how many minutes they want that specific player to get. No matter what type of numbers you have been putting up, if he plays your position, then he is getting your minutes. Period! I've seen some guys handle it better than others. Despite all the challenges, the newly branded G-league can be a great place to start a pro career because if guys are playing well but don't get called up, many can get nice deals overseas."

# OFFSEASON

College basketball teams typically start practice October 1st with games beginning in November. They culminate their seasons in March. The offseason is often closely monitored by coaches and training staff. As a professional, nobody is going to babysit you.

Whether you hire a staff of trainers specialized in enhancing a particular aspect of your game or you go at it alone, you design your own training regimen. A professional season abroad can vary in length and intensity depending on the country and how you and your agent put together the plan for the year. Many contracts in Europe will oblige you to be active for ten consecutive months, playing games from October until May or June. It's a different beast altogether from the college ranks. A contract in Asia or Australia lasts roughly seven to eight months terminating in April. Latin American league lengths vary from four to eight to ten months depending on where you are playing. These seasons can be combined

as you move from one contract to another. Keep in mind the main difference between collegiate athletics and professional athletics abroad is that there is no long-term vested interest in you as a person. A one-year or one-season contract in a foreign country is just what it sounds like. No one is concerned with your personal life. No one is concerned with how you develop in the upcoming years. They need you to be healthy and to perform for the duration of your contract. Beyond that, there is no concern. Thus, it is completely up to you to take care of your body and work on your game to be ready for your first professional training camp.

Upon entering any foreign contract as a rookie or any year of your career, it is extremely important to be healthy and in good shape. Many overseas contracts are structured, whether fully guaranteed or not, so that the team has the freedom to release you if you fail to pass physical and medical tests or to perform well in the first few days or weeks. Also, any drug habit you may have in the offseason is a personal choice, but should you fail a drug test, you will be on the first flight home.

Don't be afraid to invest in your body. Sometimes it is wise to hire a personal trainer as a rookie or to at least work out with a group of veterans who know how to train. If you stay close to your alma mater, take full advantage of the coaches and training staff who you have a relationship with and train there. If the funds or facilities are not available to you in your first offseason, just do whatever it takes to be in top physical shape once you step off the plane. Injuries are a part of sports and everyone knows that, but whether avoidable or not, arriving to a new team with an undisclosed injury or illness can cause them to void your contract immediately. Always be honest. If an offseason injury does occur, inform you agent and team. How they handle it is their choice, but if you lie or withhold information, you give them no choice. Most importantly you damage your reputation.

> Adjust your summer training program just a little going into your first professional season, no matter where it is. Ratchet up the intensity to make sure you are in great shape and ready to impress right off the plane.

> Many clubs will relocate you for the duration of the camp.

Training camp abroad can be a difficult experience for a rookie. Often times it can be difficult on veterans as well depending on the coach. European clubs are notorious for taking teams to secluded places for team building, conditioning and practices. Some teams have extensive camps, up to three weeks or more while others can accomplish the goal in four or five days. No matter how long a camp lasts in Europe, be prepared to run! Not how you ran in college, the sprints on the clock, a timed mile at the most, but real distance running. This long standing tradition for conditioning, while seen as obsolete in America, is alive and well in Europe (personal longest...1hr). Weights and basketball regimens differ from team to team, but distance running is a constant through the European leagues. Many clubs will relocate you for the duration of the camp. Living conditions vary, so bring books and your

devices. Boredom alert. Often teams in the nicer places like to move you to a remote location to allow you to focus only on getting in shape for 24 hours a day.

Preseasons differ from region to region. Preseason in Asian leagues and Australia are somewhat similar to Europe. You will be there a month or more before the season participating in preseason training and building early team chemistry. Latin countries are different with the exception of Argentina. It has its own style of play, which is a hybrid of the Latin and European markets. The preseason is highly intense and short, leaving you little time to adapt and recover, yet you still must be prepared to produce immediately. Arriving a week to ten days before the season is normal, with two weeks being a luxury, and three to five days becoming frequent. The climate is hot, the rest is less, and the game is fast paced. Less like the old eastern conference NBA teams like the Knicks or Pistons, and more like the new aged western conference teams namely the Warriors.

Long distance running can help for general endurance. However, more aggressive workouts for less time that push your lungs and muscles to aerobic and anaerobic capacity prove more suitable. Maybe trade in the treadmill for a high intensity hour of spin class. Exchange the outdoor 5-mile jogs for 8 to 10 100-meter sprints dragging a 40-pound weighted sandbag attached to your waist. Your strength sessions can also be adjusted to help change the way your body reacts. Build up power and endurance, push yourself to the limit and discover methods to rehydrate and recover quickly.

Adjust your summer training program just a little going into your first professional season, no matter where it is. Ratchet up the intensity to make sure you are in great shape and be ready to impress right off the plane. Don't be afraid to train at a new, higher level. Doing various types of workouts cause muscle confusion and create more gains, but also body soreness. As a young player, your body can take it! Do NOT show up out of shape. That is a quick way to end up back at the airport returning home, even quicker in Latin America than in Europe or Asia.

Surviving the first month or so of your rookie year abroad will entail more than just training camp and preseason "friendly" games. Be ready for extensive medical tests and numerous appointments to finalize paperwork to make sure you are eligible to play. Included in the medical test is often the aforementioned drug screening, so make good decisions in that. Most leagues will do a random screening at some point during the season. It can be on any day, or any time. FIBA rules need to be understood. Ask your team doctors about any additional doping and drug rules for your specific location. This includes supplements and medicines. Sometimes the testing can be extremely strict to the point that even NyQuil can cause a failed test. Ever heard of a player serving a suspension for trying to regrow hair

Don't be afraid to invest in your body. Sometimes it is wise to hire a personal trainer as a rookie or to at least work out with a group of veterans who know how to train.

with Rogaine? Well, apparently it contains a banned substance, so be careful and be in the know. Failing a team drug test for marijuana or recreational drugs as well as performance enhancers can sully your reputation and is not something that you want to happen during your career. Failing a league mandated test not only leaves your name tainted, but also your pockets empty. FIBA may rule that you serve at least a 2-year suspension from playing in any FIBA sanctioned league.

# LEARN THE RULES

" In FIBA, the game is the same but the rules are different. Eurosteps. Stopping fast breaks with fouls. Taking the ball off of the rim. It's a different beast altogether from the college ranks.

The globalization of the game of basketball was discussed in the introduction. The evidence of this is easy to see in the rule changes made in the international game within the last ten years. The trapezoid lane that was used until 2010 (some of you reading this may not remember, check an old Dream Team YouTube video for an example) was the standard key shape on a basketball court in international play. The NBA's wide rectangular key was considered an exception, basically an extended version of the collegiate rectangular key. Now professional basketball all over the world uses a large rectangular key, a visual symbol of the worldwide assimilation of basketball. Nonetheless, the differences in international rules cause a distinct style of play.

Overall, the rules in Europe promote a bit more methodical game. Some believe it decreases the entertainment value of the game and puts and emphasis on passing and outside shooting. No doubt Lob City of the LA Clippers, for example, does not exist without defensive three seconds. But the international game offers exciting plays in different ways. Middle pick and roll, in Europe especially, requires a minimum of two passes to get a layup or open shot because of the lack of defensive three second rule. Learning the rules beforehand can save you from a few embarrassing situations as a rookie. Also, know the 'dress code' on the court. Each league will have different rules about the accessories, braces, and types of tape you can play with. Some international competitions will hand out fines based on these violations if the player's appearance isn't changed before the jump ball.

## No defensive 3-second rule

This essentially allows the defense to keep a help defender in the lane at all times. Eliminates many first pass finishes after pick and roll, and restricts one on one play.

## No offensive goaltending

Allows a player to touch the ball while on the cylinder. Also, an offensive player can touch the ball at any time during its flight, allowing them to guide in a shot that is on the way down or sitting on the rim. It allows a defender to deflect a shot once it has touched the rim. However, on a free throw if you knock the ball in accidentally as a defender, it counts as two points. A defender cannot block a shot on its way down or once it has touched the backboard.

## Traveling

The true first step, most prevalent in Europe. This rule requires you to adhere to the 'old school' first step in which the first dribble must touch the ground before the pivot foot lifts. Often a difficult adjustment for rookies, resulting in a lot of traveling calls. Master what is known as an on-side dribble to avoid these calls. Emphasis on footwork.

## No timeout by players

Time outs may be called only by the coach and on dead balls or specified clock situations. Grab a loose ball and call timeout at ANY time of the game and it is a technical foul whether the team has timeouts or not.

"Every basketball player has the dream of playing professionally. When mine came true, it wasn't what I anticipated growing up. I always thought I would be in the NBA, never imagining that my career would start in the south of Italy. I was 21 when I signed my first contract to play in LegaDue. I knew nothing about European basketball, even less about the city I was going to call home for the next 10 months. It was a small mountain village, with a population of less than 5,000 people, situated between Rome and Naples. The town had one traffic light, small streets, wild goats and horses, the total opposite of life back in Jersey. People still washed their clothes by hand. I thought I had gone back in time, that there was no way I'd survive, until a 34-year-old vet gave some great advice that I still use today. Remain open minded he said. Stay positive and try to immerse yourself into the town and culture. Don't complain nor compare everything to life back in the states. Take advantage of the opportunities in front of you and always remember your goal. I ended up staying in that small town for 2 years. I won 2 championships and 2 MVPs. I learned Italian. I met some of my best friends there and developed values and memories that will remain with me forever. Don't overlook your options because if it wasn't for that small village, I don't think I would have as successful of a career."

Kyle Hines, PF (UNCG '08)
Passport: USA
Pro Career: Russia, Greece, Italy, Germany
3x Euroleague Champion (2012, 13, 16)
Euroleague Defensive Player of the Year
All-Euroleague Team Honorable Mention
VTB League Champion
Greek League Champion
German League Champion
German Cup Champion
German League Finals MVP
2x Italian Cup 2nd Division Champion
Italian Cup 2nd Division MVP

# KNOW THE LEAGUES

" As a rookie, it is often necessary to prove yourself before moving on to the big bucks.

# EUROPEAN LEAGUES

**The highest level of play in Europe is the Euroleague, which is the best basketball in the world outside of the NBA. In between the Euroleague level and entry-level leagues, there are many levels of play and salary in Europe.**

» **The best basketball outside of the NBA!**

The level of play throughout Europe varies from league to league. Some countries such as Norway, Finland, Denmark, Sweden, Holland, Portugal and Switzerland are excellent places to live but the level of these leagues is not so high. Do not look down upon them! As a rookie, it is often necessary to prove yourself before moving on to the big bucks. Leagues such as these are stepping stones. They provide great opportunities and places to live for young Americans. At all player positions, they allow you to show your skills, as well as build your stats and resume.

Spain and Italy are traditionally the best leagues in Europe for the past few decades. Greece was at the top of that list but due to their economic decline, there hasn't been enough money available to attract the same level of players that it once had. These leagues have produced many NBA stars. In recent years, Germany and especially Turkey have risen to the top of the strongest leagues as well. The Euroleague however, is a combination of the top 16 teams in all of Europe. The teams all have large budgets, private planes, huge arenas, commercials and regularly televised games.     A player that achieves a high level of success in the Euroleague is automatically on the radar for an NBA job. Some players have even been known to forego NBA contracts for those offered by Euroleague teams depending on the situation.

Outside of the Euroleague there is what is known as the Eurocup and other international competitions. Where as Euroleague is top tier, Eurocup is considered the second-tier transnational professional basketball competition, compiling of the next best 24 teams in Europe. Trickling down from these are other similarly formatted leagues such as the Champions League, FIBA EuropeCup, ABA League (former Adriatic League) and VTB League. All of these leagues allow you to compete on a team that participates in the league of its own country as well as against similar caliber teams from other countries. They are very valuable on a resume and exciting, as you will be traveling to another country each week to play. This also broadens your appeal as a player and introduces you to other markets.

# ASIAN LEAGUES

**The level of play in Asia differs from Europe. For the most part, players are less developed physically and may lack the level of basketball education structure implemented in Europe.**

You are only as strong as your weakest link. For local players, the exposure to the highest levels of basketball competition may be less. This possibly hinders some from growing to the potential performance level of a European player.

However, many Asian businesses have long served as renowned sponsors for some of the clubs. All of these leagues are great places to do what you love to do and make money doing it. Although also employing guards, Asian markets can be seen as immediate destination targets for big men. The demographics indicate that the majority of Asians are either short or tall in comparison to other ethnicities. A solid big man can potentially earn an excellent living there. China is the front-runner financially for contracting the big boys but Iran and the

Philippines, among others, can be great opportunities. The consistent contract securities that can be gained in the Japanese and Korean markets make for solid careers.

The two main international Asian competitions are the Asian Club and Arab Club Championships. They are Asia's spin-offs of Euroleague, putting top clubs in their markets against one another, competing for the Cup. The teams participating in these competitions are usually known to sign a player or two if their regular season is not running at that time. You may be signed only to compete for that specified period. ASEAN League and WABA League are smaller, more regionally concentrated, Asian competitions. Consistently explore all playing options.

# LATIN LEAGUES

Level of play has its own class in Latin countries. In the better of these leagues, many players are developed physically, but are not as big. These players are built in an aggressive, streamlined concept. They are explosively fast and athletic, which is perfect for their "NBA-like" structured calendar of three or four games per week. Argentina is one of the top leagues in the Latin world. It assimilates the European market in their season structure, half-court style of play and the physical development of their players. Countries like Puerto Rico (albeit a U.S. territory), Dominican Republic, Venezuela and Brazil are guard heavy, faster leagues where as Mexico and the aforementioned Argentina are slower with more local big men.

The more frequent signings in these countries are versatile players that can move extremely well up and down the floor. Contrary to European markets, being a proven scorer is a must, as there is a saying in Latin leagues, "It is better to be Jordan than to be Pippen." With shorter, quicker seasons, with the exception of Argentina and Mexico, these Latin markets give you more flexibility as to how you put together your year as a player. Contracts are shorter and less guaranteed than in Europe and Asia. This possibly allows you to move to two or three destinations in a year's time, at you or your team's discretion. This comes at a price of many games played and wear and tear on your body (personal best 112 games within 12 months). It is imperative that you stay healthy.

Liga de Las Americas, another regional-adjusted rendition of Euroleague, is the top international competition between the best 16 teams of all of the Latin American leagues. Liga Sudamericana, which is based on the same concept, is limited to the best 16 teams only from South American countries.

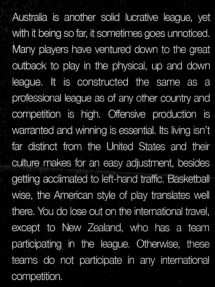

Australia is another solid lucrative league, yet with it being so far, it sometimes goes unnoticed. Many players have ventured down to the great outback to play in the physical, up and down league. It is constructed the same as a professional league as of any other country and competition is high. Offensive production is warranted and winning is essential. Its living isn't far distinct from the United States and their culture makes for an easy adjustment, besides getting acclimated to left-hand traffic. Basketball wise, the American style of play translates well there. You do lose out on the international travel, except to New Zealand, who has a team participating in the league. Otherwise, these teams do not participate in any international competition.

# OTHER LEAGUES

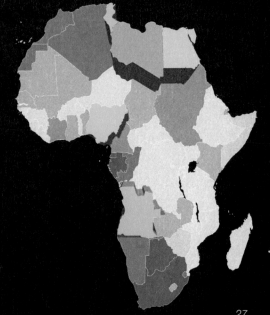

African leagues provide very few opportunities for decent play, the majority being in Angola, Tunisia and Nigeria. These leagues can be researched by your agent should you urge to venture that way. With few exceptions, local players in these regions rely more on athletic talent than skill. You will have many responsibilities as an import player. Libya also was once a habited league, whose landscape has changed since the downfall of Gaddafi. The African Champions Cup is the international competition involving the top 10 teams in Africa.

# NOTES

TIP: Compare the style and level of player you are with the successful players in the different leagues around the world. Learn where you too can maximize your earning potential.

_____

_____

_____

_____

_____

_____

_____

_____

_____

_____

_____

_____

*__Don't forget to chronicle your journey with us at myhoopjourney.com__*

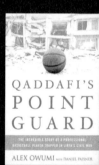

QADDAFI'S
POINT
GUARD

THE INCREDIBLE STORY OF A PROFESSIONAL
BASKETBALL PLAYER TRAPPED IN LIBYA'S CIVIL WAR

ALEX OWUMI with DANIEL PAISNER

"A lot of people focus on the negatives of being a professional basketball player overseas, but for me I want to focus on a couple of my positives from my time in Europe. The first one for me is the style of play and the way the rules are different from America. Most of the teams I have played on focus on the half-court game and they run their plays all the way through. As a shooter this benefits me because I like to come off of screens and focus on where I can get my open shots. The second, is the relationship I've had with team managers and coaches. I've been fortunate to come across and play for great managers and coaches who have made my transition really easy for me in Europe. These are relationships I keep this very day and hopefully can help me in the future."

*Alex Owumi, PG (Alcorn St. '08)*
*Passport: USA/Nigeria*
*Pro Career: UK, Middle East, France*
*Author of 'Qaddafi's Point Guard'*

# LIVING THE LIFESTYLE

> Take advantage and learn some history. Take some pictures. Create memories. Try the local cuisine.

In your first few days overseas you've probably been dragged around to see a medical doctor, orthopedist, and cardiologist, been to a local government office, the team office, visa appointments, moved into your new apartment or home, etc. To cap it all off, you still have jet lag. Needless to say, the first week abroad can be a bit uncomfortable and tiring once you couple all of these responsibilities with playing basketball. Keep in mind that if you are playing well and are punctual to your appointments, once you return from training camp, you will have settled into a nice routine. Your sleep pattern will adjust naturally and you should quickly master the layout of the city you are in. Using your phone or purchasing a GPS can

expedite this process. Either way you are in a new country, employed as a professional basketball player. What could be better! Take advantage of the opportunity you have.

Keeping a positive mindset and accepting your surroundings is important. And once again, recognize the opportunities at your fingertips. Basketball is the priority, and the tool around which you will build a resume, reputation and elevate your lifestyle. However, living abroad offers other means of enhancing you personally and gaining assets that cannot be measured in dollars and cents. Use the opportunity to learn about the country you are in as well as teaching family. Allowing relatives to come abroad to experience your day-to-day life can be priceless for both parties. At the moment, you are getting a chance to see the world. You never know what obstacles and challenges life will bring you, or whether you will ever get the opportunity to return to experience that country again. Wherever you are, it will have a richer history than any American city based on age alone. Take advantage and learn some history. Take some pictures. Create memories. Remember to be open-minded and that the American way is not the only way. Don't always look for the nearest burger or slice of pizza. Try the local cuisine. Whether it is souvlaki in Greece, sancocho if you are in Dominican Republic, or kangaroo meat when down in Aussie land, it can be an enriching and flavorful experience.

Broaden your horizon. The experience is what's valuable. You are now a "foreigner". Be respectful to local customs, greetings and traditions. Learn them. It's an easy way to gain friends and be respected by the locals. Kudos if you decide to delve deep enough in the culture to learn the language! While this can be challenging and time consuming, learning a foreign language is invaluable in many industries. It will be easier to learn a language while living there than any other time. Take advantage if possible. It will also help you communicate with coaches, teammates and staff who may not speak English.

Language is not the only thing you can pursue to learn. American accredited universities are frequent around the world, offering opportunities through online and local enrollment programs. These schools offer undergraduate and post-graduate classes in English. Unexplainably selfish, it is known that in the United States, we tend to be mostly concerned about what is happening in our own country. In Europe, for example, citizens in one country may know as much if not more about a neighboring country than we may know about a neighboring state. If further education is important to you and online classes aren't your forte, this can prove to be a viable option to learn on a greater world scale. If feasible, research the local American university and the programs it offers. Most colleges have two types of eight-week programs for certain degrees like an MBA (Masters of Business Administration). For example, one offering of classes may be from Monday through Thursday evenings for the conventional student. The same exact eight-week program may be offered, doubled in hours, coupled in a Friday evening and half-day Saturday format. This schedule is catered those that have other obligations during the week. Talk to your team management to help you figure out how to fit this into your practice and game schedule. Manage your time wisely and stay focused, and you may be able to go home with more than just a championship.

Don't be afraid to break the mold of the typical American athlete. In general, arrogance, ignorance, small mindedness, cockiness and selfishness are all words that are used to describe American athletes abroad. These stereotypes vary from place to place, but they are ever present and sometimes justified. Build good relationships within your club, with fans, and with management. Embrace and enjoy the culture you are surrounded by. Having a solid reputation off the court is valuable when combined with solid on court performance. Just like any other job, it's good to have people like the work you do and it's even better if they like the person you are. This is the way to get re-offered contracts with your team. Information about players' personalities and coach-ability is shared just as freely as are your stats and film. Build your reputation on and off the court while effectively and efficiently using your surroundings to grow as a person.

> Keeping a positive mindset and accepting your surroundings are important. Recognize the opportunities at your fingertips.

# THE "HUMP"

We've all heard of hump day even if we have not experienced it yet. Perhaps you've heard your parents talking about being tired, burnt out and lacking motivation on a Wednesday, just hoping to make it over the proverbial hump. Think of your season the same way, except in basketball, you may run into hump months. These times are more evident for players in countries with longer seasons, Europe and the Eastern world. In shorter Latin leagues where the games are numerous, you may run into a hump week, which is considered more of a short slump. Homesickness is similar but not as bad as you are much closer to home since you are technically still in the "Americas". Also, after a bad game, the rumors get loud quickly, placing pressure on your shoulders. However, with a few games a week versus only having one, you have a chance to redeem yourself sooner. If you catch the big hump in those countries, it can be considered a bad season. Getting back on track is important to keep jobs, and may be done with the right focus and outlook. Clear your head and get back in the gym!

Europe is a whole different beast. In a typical European season, it usually begins in November. Perhaps you have been with your team since August or September and there is nothing more you would like to do than be watching college football and eating Thanksgiving dinner with family. Maybe the weather is beginning to get cold and your body is getting tired from the pounding of preseason and the high intensity of the first round of league games. This usually brings on the struggle months. Not all leagues allot time for players to fly home for the holidays. You may spend Christmas and/or New Year's Eve with your teammates or alone. Be prepared to deal with a feeling of physical fatigue that you may not be accustomed to and remember its 90% mental. Just get over the hump!

Keep in mind that these down times in the season can be detrimental to your play. Mental toughness will be asked of you at this point. The New Year marks the mid-point of most European leagues and is a perfect time for them to replace players who are not performing well. Do not let your play slide! If you have to have your family come visit you or whatever you have to do to tough it out, make sure your performance is consistent year round.

Some, rookies especially, may experience severe homesickness and decide to leave teams early. It can be debilitating if bad enough. Just take your time with your decision and keep your future in mind. Don't underestimate your mental fortitude. If you stick it out, you will get over it. Remember, your reputation precedes you throughout your basketball career and leaving a team early may represent instability to some coaches. Using some of the tips from the previous section and acclimating yourself into your surroundings will help tremendously. Try your best to keep your head clear. Ships sink because of the water that gets IN them, not because of the water around them. Don't let too much get inside of you and weigh you down. Trust me, at the end of your first season you will look back on it and say it flew by!

# GETTING OUT AND ABOUT

Hopefully your season goes smoothly and you enjoy your location while performing well and staying healthy. Ideal situation. Add a healthy social life to that and you've had a great year on and off the court. We all know the possibilities of social life as a collegiate athlete. Not going into any details, the same elements exist everywhere in the world. The extra attention that you get as a professional is much greater than what you were used to in college. Regardless, we all have social lives on different scales and so as not to sound like a parent, remember the word 'reputation.' Again, your reputation is more valuable than any numbers that you can put up.

Outside of the U.S.A., partying and socializing can have very different levels. Different cultures have different views on sex, alcohol, and even different laws than you are used to. For example, in the United States, the blood alcohol limit is 0.08%. In Poland, they take being drunk to a much higher level. A blood alcohol content of 0.02% can get your license suspended for six months to three years, not to mention up to one month in prison. That's literally two beers. Goodbye Sunday football with the boys. If you

were to go further than that and blow a 0.05% blood alcohol content, you can get your drivers license banned for a minimum of three years, plus up to three years behind bars. Oh, you thought you and a new lady friend were going to have a late night out drinking on the town? Keep it Uber. In Poland, the amount of alcohol that our American society deems as harmless can damage your reputation, your quality of life and cause you to lose your job.

Know the rules, know what is socially acceptable, and know what is expected of you by your organization. Is the coach or president of a certain religion that he is offended by alcohol consumption? Don't drink at team functions. Are age limits different for young women to enter nightclubs where you are? Be careful! Does your contract have a curfew for the night or two nights before a game? Read the fine print. The common sense that has gotten you to this point will serve you well abroad as long as you know the rules. Follow them and be responsible, and you won't allow your social life to damage your reputation.

# LET'S TALK MONEY

> You've got to start at the bottom. Patience and performance. The money will come.

As young athletes, we all dream of making the big bucks. Some hit the lotto right away. Others never break even. Same deal in the international basketball market. Coming out of college as an undrafted rookie, you may receive some international offers for more money than you could have ever imagined. However, many are disappointed by the harsh reality that just like any other college graduate entering the workforce in an entry-level position, you've got to start at the bottom. When faced with this, players tend to compare themselves to other players' contracts. They don't understand the market so they begin to blame and immediately switch agents, thinking the grass is greener on the other side. If you have done your homework like we mentioned back in the agent section, and really trust the process you took in choosing him, these doubts shouldn't weigh as much on you. On the bright side (and the dark side), the international basketball market is extremely volatile salary wise. With good stats and consistent performance on winning teams your value can grow exponentially. For example, if you make $20k as a rookie, you can triple that easily each of your first few seasons. Which means, in only your third season you are already a six-figure player. For all of you math majors, imagine if you start at 50k, 75k and up. Patience and performance will lead to success.

However, things work even faster in reverse. Unlike the NBA where a 3-year rookie deal is the standard and a five-year max deal is the goal for an all-star caliber player, internationally, contracts are typically one year or one season at a time. This means an injury or a bad season, personal problems or a losing team, can all adversely affect the salary level you have reached. Find the balance between I and team

> As young athletes, we all dream of making the big bucks. Some hit the lotto right away. Others never break even.

In professional basketball everyone has an agenda, and you should as well. To advance your career is your number one goal. Your stats are like your business card.

Before a coach sees what you look like or your film, they see your numbers. Make sure your numbers reflect a complete game, not just points per. Keep your percentages high, assist-to-turnover ratio efficient and a solid overall evaluation. And WIN! Don't forget that your team's wins and losses reflect on you personally. Any hint of selfishness may affect your outlook in different ways depending on where you are playing. Winning is the end game, everyone wants a winner. In Asia, they want you to lead. In Latin leagues, they want you to score and win. In Europe, it is much easier to build a career as a guy who scores ten points a game and wins championships, than a twenty point per game volume scorer who plays on bad teams. Know where you are playing, what the team needs from you, and find the balance. But one thing to remember is winning trumps all.

"We play basketball for the love of the game but when you are a professional, you also play for the money. Money problems can be the most frustrating thing to go through with any team. Reading your contracts all the way to the fine print can assist you in knowing your rights. Don't only depend on your agent. Find ways to protect yourselves and keep your agent aware of everything happening financially with your team. Staying on top of these things can be the difference in you getting all of your money and leaving disappointed with pockets empty. Acting reckless can only make the situation worse. I have had to contract services of a lawyer before, as well as print up my own promissory notes and get them signed by the team owner. You work hard for your money. Achieving your money can only be a few legitimate steps away. Remain professional but be persistent and get what you came for."

*James Maye, SG/SF (UNCG '03)*
*Passport: USA/Dominican Republic*
*Pro Career: Everywhere: Europe, Asia, Latin America,*
*Australia, Africa*
*Co-Author: The Journeyman's Guide*
*Bio in the About the Authors section*

# KNOW YOUR WORTH

Stay aware of your money matters when abroad. Currency exchange rates and wiring fees cause confusion for players abroad. Make sure that you know whether your contract value is stated in US dollars or in foreign currency. Also, keep track of the exchange rate throughout the year. Rates are forever changing.

Be aware of every transaction you make abroad. If you use an American debit card in a foreign ATM, you will be charged a fee. The amount depends on your specific bank. The fees may or may not be mentioned on the ATM screen. When making an in-store purchase with an American card, you will see a 'foreign transaction fee' on your bank or credit card statement.

Before using your American card overseas, you should contact your card-issuing bank and let them know where and when you will be traveling, and for how long. Many banks will block your card if they sense possible fraud or card theft. They do this to protect themselves and more so, to protect you. Contacting your bank from international territory to resolve a blocked card issue can be very frustrating for you as a player.

This takes time and verification of both identity and transaction history. In many cases, they will issue a new card, which may leave you without funds for numerous days.

When entering into the United States, you are not allowed to carry $10,000 or more in currency without declaring it. If you don't and are caught, you may have to forfeit the money and face civil and or criminal penalties.

Opening an account in the country in which you live is a feasible way to avoid some of these debacles. Check with your team to make sure the banking system in your country is reliable! The economic climate of some countries can be volatile and put your money in jeopardy.

Stay in the know! It will avoid some embarrassing moments. It can prevent the shock of sending your money home and seeing a number that you didn't expect. A player was once escorted out of a Belarusian strip club after thinking he had generously tipped the ladies with 100,000 Rubles. It looks like a lot of money. It can be intimidating to be in a foreign country and have to withdraw local currency in 6 or 7 figure chunks just for one night out on the town. Even worse is being hastily removed from an establishment by Belarusian bouncers for tipping the equivalent of $5 for a full night of entertainment. Don't let the numbers fool you. Know its true value.

A common issue with international basketball is late or missing payments. Unlike the NBA, international leagues have much more financial flux. A league may start with 20 teams and finish with only 18. Teams may have their funds cut off by sponsors or owners. They may release players. They may even go bankrupt. In any of these cases, players may miss multiple paychecks or be released without pay. In some countries, you never have to worry about receiving the salary that you signed for. You will get every dime. In others, you may only receive a partial amount of the money owed to you with little or no way to recover the rest. This often happens in countries with economic problems, such as Greece over the last few years.

Germany and France have legal processes and government protection for situations like these. Smaller Western European countries and many Asian countries are considered to be secure financially and trustworthy as a whole. Eastern European, Mediterranean and Middle Eastern countries are places where you need to research the reputation of each individual team. NOT many Latin leagues offer guaranteed contracts. Due to

> DO NOT leave the country without your money or at least setting up something binding in order to receive your money.

the harsh schedule, it allows teams to quickly change players without economic repercussions. They may only guarantee your money up until your last day of official participation with the team. If you are cut midseason, you will only be paid up until that day, not for the full season. Be sure to check the wording on your contract.

FIBA has a system in place in case you do have a serious problem receiving the money owed to you from your team. Requests for arbitration can be sent to the FIBA Basketball Arbitral Tribunal, which is based in Switzerland. There are some costs associated with going through FIBA Arbitration. To start, there is a non-reimbursable handling fee of 1,500 euros for any disputes for sums up to 30,000 euros, a fee of 2,000 euros for disputes between 30,001 and 100,000 euros, and upwards from there. Again, those are administration charges.

The legal fees, however, are refundable. You can expect to come out of pocket anywhere between 5,000 and 7,000 euros during the total process in order to get the money owed to you. The whole FIBA arbitration process can be resolved within 3 to 6 months.

One last tip! If the team causes you to have any doubt about receiving your salary and you are not fully protected legally either by your contract or FIBA, DO NOT leave the country without your money or at least setting up something binding in order to receive your money. Even a promissory note conceding the debt, signed by both you and the team, can be a valid option. Whatever you decide to set up, be sure there is wording stating that the owner is personally responsible for the debt and not just the team. A team can claim bankruptcy, change its name, and continue without ever paying to you what you're owed. If you fly without taking any action, you are then leaving it up to the team or club to be the honest guys. If they were already that, then you would have had no problem getting your money up to that point. Once again...stay in the know and know your worth!

> Teams sometimes go bankrupt, release players and have their funds cut off by sponsors or owners. In this case players can be released without pay, or miss multiple paychecks.

# NOTES

TIP: Keep record of your pay schedule and the exchange rates, Some teams pay you in their country's currency. Know exactly what you are owed and when.

_____

_____

_____

_____

_____

_____

_____

_____

_____

_____

_____

_____

***Don't forget to chronicle your journey with us at myhoopjourney.com***

# OBTAINING A FOREIGN PASSPORT

> A foreign passport can open up options for you to experience things on a scale you may never have as an American.

# DUAL-CITIZENSHIP

It is not uncommon for an American player to receive a foreign passport and thus enhancing their value as a player in that country.

All leagues governed by FIBA have rules on how many import and domestic players can be on each roster. This adds value to players with passports that are most commonly accepted. Some players are lucky enough to have a family member within a generation or two, whose bloodline may allow them to gain access to foreign citizenship through the lineage. Again, those are the lucky ones. If not, there are a few very general ways to get a passport, none of which are easy and all of which require you to be a high level player with a great reputation in that country.

Laws vary from country to country, region to region, continent to continent. In all of these manners of attempting to achieve a second passport, there will be many legal obstacles as well as political ones. Your agent, your team, the strength of their connections and your level of play will be the main influencers in how efficient, if at all possible, this process will be. If attainable, the amount that holding dual citizenship can positively enhance your career is immeasurable.

**Marriage:** If you marry a citizen of a particular country, you most likely can apply for residency and eventually citizenship based on the laws permitting you to adjoin your lives as a married couple. If children are included in the scenario, the process may become quicker or more technical, based on that country's laws.

**Presidential Discretion:** The President of some countries may have the power to grant citizenship to up to four people per calendar year. A team that has strong government ties may be able to use that political influence to naturalize you. A high level of performance on the court can increase your chances. That country's basketball federation can present to you and the President the idea of you playing for their Men's National Team, thus assisting them in representing their flag in front of the world.

**Residency:** After a few years of playing consistently in the same country, you may be able to apply for residency based on the amount of time you have spent in that country as an upstanding non-citizen. After obtaining residency, there may be other required steps before taking that country's oath and achieving full citizenship.

There are a few important classes of passports that you want to be aware of. Bosman A players are those that hold passports to European Union countries plus Switzerland. Bosman B players have passports from any other European country. These are mostly Eastern European countries, including Israel and Turkey. In some countries, there is also a rule that benefits Cotonou players. These players hold passports from any country included in the African, Caribbean, and Pacific Group of States (ACP).

Not only does obtaining dual citizenship free yourself from absolute dependence in one country, it opens a door for you to lengthen your basketball career. Think of it like this. In general, let's take a random Western European team where the rule in their league may be that out of 12 players, you can have 2 true foreigners, 4 Bosmans and six locals. Along with your agent, check your lineage and birthplace to see if you qualify for a foreign or Bosman passport, and in which markets it may hold value. As an American, you would occupy one of the two true foreigner spots. With a European passport, you are likely able to occupy one of the Bosman spots. If you happen to hold a passport for that particular country you are playing in, you may occupy a true local spot. Certain countries, like Spain or France, may have additional rules regarding Cotonou passport holders. A person decent in math can easily see how there is an immediate increase in the probability of you getting a job once obtaining a second passport in the right place. These laws are constantly changing from league to league.

> Obtaining dual citizenship opens a door for you to lengthen your basketball career.

In Latin countries, for the most part, leagues have their locals plus a two or three import player rule. A Bosman passport doesn't apply here. A communitary rule in Latin countries allow the teams to roster an additional player holding any Caribbean passport. By the end of 2016, Puerto Rico was the only league still using the rule, however, they have since abolished it for the 2017 season.

Here is a simpler breakdown similar to the European one above. Let's say the team can have only two foreigners and ten locals to make up the twelve-man roster. As you age, contrary to your knowledge of the game, your body will slowly diminish. Time always wins. As a foreigner, the competition will become higher with the fresh wave of younger players emerging as frontrunners for those jobs. With a second passport, you will have less pressure to continue to be "the man" as your game wears away. As long as you prove valuable to your team, they can continue to keep you without the stress of you having to be one of the two best players on the team just to keep money coming in. You can simply take a role as a sixth man, energy guy or locker-room leader.

A foreign passport can open up options for you to experience things on a scale you may never have as an American, like playing with another country's National Team on the world stage. If applied correctly, obtaining dual citizenship can help solidify the stature of your career by lengthening it and allowing you to bow out a little more gracefully as you slide further and further towards the end of the bench. In those extended years, you may use the time wisely to develop relationships on and off the court effectively. This valuable time can also allow you to figure out a post-basketball career in double markets without as much financial pressure, while you are still capable of collecting a check playing.

*All information regarding passports can and should be researched within FIBA as to know which passports to pursue and where they will prove most useful for your career.*

Not only does obtaining dual citizenship free yourself from absolute dependence on one country, it opens a door for you to lengthen your basketball career.

Ronnie Burrell, PF (UNCG '05)
Passport: USA
Pro Career: France, Germany, Poland
Co-Author: The Journeyman's Guide
Bio in the About the Authors section

"One of my vets told me early in my career to always be friends with the trainer. One story from my time in Poland, we had a very good trainer who was a hard worker but was severely underpaid. We became friends and I knew that he liked to drink vodka, maybe a little too much. I personally don't like vodka but I always kept a bottle of Nemiroff in my apartment. He was on call for me 24 hours a day. Late night arrival after a road trip, he would bring his table to my house for a massage if I wanted, 2am, 3am, didn't matter. If I was sick and needed medicine or an IV, I never had to leave my house. He would deliver anything to me at any time. I'm not sure if he just liked me that much or he just wanted the free drink, but he kept my body performing at a high level for three Euroleague seasons in Poland."

# NO PAIN, NO PAIN...

A continued positive bill of health of the players can be a main factor in whether a team succeeds or fails. The trainers and team doctors are in charge of keeping the numbers on the court at a maximum and those in the training room low.

Injuries are, and have always been, a scary but inevitable part of sports. Dealing with them outside of your comfort zone only compounds the problems. There are many factors to consider when dealing with an injury abroad. The main piece of advice to remember is that, if at all possible, have an old college team doctor or personal doctor that you can reach out to for a second opinion. If you don't have one, contact other professional athletes you know for recommendations of a reputable one. It is important to have someone in your corner that cares about you personally and has no agenda, whereas a team doctor almost always has one. Some agendas are personal and simply deal with them wanting to maintain a good professional reputation. In this case it is good for the athlete, as you can expect quality treatment and an accurate diagnosis.

> It is YOUR body. Make the decisions that you are comfortable with, especially if surgery is involved.

Injuries are, and have always been, a scary but inevitable part of sports. It is important to have someone in your corner that cares about you personally and has no agenda.

Some team doctors feel pressure from the coaches or management to prescribe the quick fix, instead of the best solution to your injury for your future. Vitamins, anti-inflammatories and corticosteroids are the most common recommended treatments if conventional therapy, ultrasound, and other modalities have proven unsuccessful. They sound well, but the truth is, depending on your injury, this can reduce pain but escalate the problem. This is when it is appropriate to get a copy of your x-rays, MRI or whatever the case may be, and send it to the aforementioned trusted doctor. It is YOUR body. Make the decisions that you are comfortable with, especially if surgery is involved. Some of the best doctors and surgeons in the world are found outside of the United States and depending on your teams' accessibility to them, you can get great treatment. While on the other hand, some countries are simply places where you do not want to go under the knife for any reason unless completely necessary. Ask other players about the doctor's credibility and skill. If you sustain a serious injury that incapacitates you, never hesitate to fly family over to help you, consult other doctors or make it back to the States where you are more comfortable.

Make sure that your agent closely reads your contract so that you are clear on the type of insurance you will be given in whatever country you may be headed to. As in all of our topics, there is a broad spectrum of possible scenarios ranging from full coverage for any and everything with no expense to you, to absolutely no insurance what so ever. Know your insurance status.

# YOUR LOVED ONES

> Being able to expose a family member or friend, who has not had the opportunity to travel, can be priceless.

Many countries, mostly in Europe and maybe Asia, offer the opportunity for you and your entire family to be insured. In most markets, you may be provided living arrangements, car and flights to accommodate your children and spouse. Be sure to ask the management of your team about these during contract negotiations. If they really want you as a player and are financially able, you will be surprised what things you can get added to your contract. Even if you are not married, you may be able to get flights for your girlfriend or family.

It also can be invaluable to raise children abroad. Your city may have daycares or schools that will accommodate them, allowing them the opportunity to pick up a foreign language with ease. Using foreign insurance to pay for the birth of your child is not always a bad idea also. Most countries are appalled at the lack of good health and maternity coverage in America and for good reason. These things are often much more affordable abroad. As long as the woman is comfortable with the medical treatment, it can be a great experience. Just be mindful of the dates as far as health concerns with flying and consult your team and doctors.

Dealing with a family emergency, death in the family or wanting to attend important events (weddings, graduations etc.) can be tricky when thousands of miles from home. Obviously some events are simply more important than basketball and take precedence and the team will excuse you. The most important thing when traveling is making sure you have constant availability to your family, whether on the road or at home. It is important that you educate your family, especially older members, on how to use the proper technology to contact you. Be sure to get a SIM card/phone chip in whatever country you are in to have a local number immediately. Unlocking your American phone to accommodate the foreign chip will save you money from having to buy a second phone. You can speak with your phone service carrier or order the unlock code for your specific phone from outside sources. With all the technology used nowadays, you won't miss a beat, as most of your apps only need an Internet signal to function. You never know when an emergency arises. Also, inform family members of the charges related to international phone calls and texts that are not through the Internet. For some parents and grandparents, these concepts are not always second nature.

Being able to expose a family member or friend, who has not had the opportunity to travel, can be priceless. As part of your personal growth in a foreign country, don't be afraid to share the experience with family and friends if you are able.

> If they really want you as a player and are financially able, you will be surprised what things you can get added to your contract.

*Courtney Eldridge, PG (UNCG '02)*
*Passport: USA*
*Pro Career: Poland, Italy, Turkey, Belarus,*
*Brazil, Dominican Republic*
*Top 8 Euroleague*

"It's important to budget the amount of money you're going to spend every month, a reasonable budget within your means, and have the discipline to stay there. During the season, things will be fine because you have a steady flow of income. It's the off-season spending that will have you like " damn, where did all my money go?" The majority of professional basketball players don't often plan on working in the summer unless you're lucky or unlucky (depending on who you're asking) enough to score a gig in a country where they play during those months. We often spend time with loved ones, working out, and doing things we can't do while we are abroad. I travelled, got bottle service at clubs and bought designer clothes in addition to my regular expenses. I had some really expensive habits. I enjoyed the prime of my life but was living season to season, the equivalent of a person with a regular job living check to check. Not to discourage anyone from treating themselves to nice things and vacation, but at the end of your career you don't want to have made X amount of dollars and have nothing to show for it. If possible, have your agent negotiate a per win bonus in your contract. Win 3 or 4 games that month, and there's your budgeted allowance right there. You'll be saving all of your "salary" for that month. A few months like that, coupled with adhering to your budget, will have you in a much better position at the end of each season."

CHECK
YOUR$ELF

# PERSONAL FINANCE

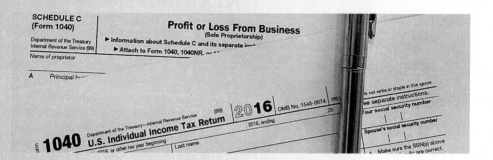

The idea that athletes live overly extravagant lifestyles is overused in my opinion. Financial issues are universal and no one is an exception. However, as an athlete, you will experience all of the things you have seen and heard about. Friends and family wanting money. The urge to splurge. Helping those who may or may not need a few dollars. Business proposals and bad investments. Wanting to enhance your own lifestyle in different ways. This is something that you will not be a stranger to as an athlete.

Playing abroad does not offer long-term security and may require a bit more care and careful planning than other career paths. Hiring a financial advisor is often a good decision if you have no experience with foreign currency or personal finance. Quick tip! Always know the value of your local currency, the exchange rate, and how you are paid. Rates fluctuate from month to month and can affect your bottom line.

Everyone has different needs and habits. But remember, following the actions of peers and other athletes can get you in trouble. Don't assume that someone who is your counterpart and lives a certain lifestyle is making good decisions. Not everyone is honest about his or her income nor is it important. Live a lifestyle that you are comfortable with, unaffected by your surroundings.

The common misconception is that all money made overseas is tax-free. Tax 'free' is not necessarily true, but close. You will essentially pay taxes on your money in whatever country you are. The team will take the taxes out before paying you. For example, if your contract says you will make $20 net, the team will be paying $25 dollars gross and pay the $5 tax to its local authority before you even see it. It is your responsibility to keep all of your documentation and paperwork from your team. Bring it home and file taxes in America. You will receive what is known as a foreign tax credit or exemption. Not all accountants may be aware of this rule so find the right one. Using deductions, or filing yourself as your own business through sole proprietorship, may have its tax advantages.

You need to know that playing professional basketball is a business. Yes, you are a business. So as a self-employed sole proprietor, you can deduct certain expenses from your business income in calculating profits for tax purposes. There are two major things you must keep in mind. One, the expenses must be determined "ordinary" and "necessary" in order for you to carry out the business of playing professional basketball. Two, you need to show substantiation. This means you must be able to prove that these expenses were paid or incurred during the taxable year. Expenses purposed wholly and exclusively for the sport of playing basketball are entirely deductible. If there is a multi-purpose expense where a portion of it is incurred specifically for your profession, that part can also be deducted.

Here are some common examples of things that may be deducted in whole or in part, but limited to each individual case. Agent, managerial, accounting, tax preparation and legal fees related to your business are all deductible items. Training fees purposed after injuries or for your upkeep as a professional player are as well. These are things such as hiring a personal trainer, masseuse, chiropractor or physical therapist. These may also include expenses related to the rental, purchase, and insurance of training equipment, training facility, and gym access. Even nutritional supplements qualify as they contribute to you as an athlete staying in "good physical condition"

> Stick to reasonable expenses that are commonly accepted. This will help you avoid most red flags at tax time.

54

> You must be able to show substantiation of expenses which are determined ordinary and necessary in order for you to carry out the business of playing professional basketball.

as usually required by your contracts. Players fail to remember expenses like the purchase of clothing and shoes labeled as professional clothing or telephone and Internet costs of being abroad. Transportation to and from practices, games, training facilities, events, and competitions related to your profession are all tax-deductible expenses and often neglected. There are many other lesser items. Professional subscriptions and journals, research assistance and material like the purchase of this book, and bank overdraft fees are such.

Here's a general hint! Stick to reasonable expenses that are commonly accepted in the business of professional basketball. This will help you avoid most red flags at tax time. As an average income earner and spender, it may be easier to keep records such as individual receipts. For those of you really maxing out your earnings as a professional player, you may have other sponsorships or contracts related. It may be in your best interest to open a separate bank account to help distinguish between your personal and professional activities. It will allow you to keep a clearer and more detailed business record of what comes in and goes out.

A thorough accountant will know all of these things. Make sure you file taxes and stay on top of it. Trust me, the reach of the IRS is long. You do not want to receive a large tax bill for misreported or unfiled income. Once you want to purchase a home, your taxes must be up to date and in order.

Planning your finances through a season can be tricky since you most likely won't get paid in the offseason. Do not rush into decisions such as purchasing homes and automobiles. These are things that we all want for ourselves early in our careers, however, what will they be used for while you are away in season? There is nothing wrong with renting or using corporate housing in the offseason. Stay with family as a young athlete as long as possible! This may not seem cool, but in hindsight, saving as much as you can early on is always best. Lastly, remember it is your money that you've earned and don't be quick to give it away. Many people have a false sense of how much money professional athletes make and will not hesitate to ask. You are starting out young and doing what you love to do so have fun and enjoy the life, but remember, there is a life after basketball that you will eventually need money for. Do not develop unhealthy patterns or relationships in which you are handing out money on a regular basis. This has been the financial downfall of many athletes that we all know well. There is nothing further to discuss here, as all of the information is well documented in modern media. Take your time and make smart decisions.

> Don't assume that someone who is your counterpart and lives a certain lifestyle is making good decisions. Start to invest in your future and save with the first check you earn as a pro.

# NOTES

TIP: Log expenditures. Research potential financial advisors and tax preparers that can assist you with taxes and in keeping your budget intact.

_____

_____

_____

_____

_____

_____

_____

_____

_____

_____

***Don't forget to chronicle your journey with us at myhoopjourney.com***

*Marcus Faison, SG/SF (Siena '00)*
*Passport: USA, Belgium*
*Belgium National Team 2010-12*
*Pro Career: Spain, Greece, Belgium, Ukraine, Turkey,*
*Germany, Georgia, Philippines, Iran, Georgia, Finland*
*11 years top international competitions*
*(2 Euroleague, 7 ULEB, 2 Eurochallenge)*
*Euroleague Final Four*

"One of the biggest misconceptions as an American playing overseas is that you don't have to report the income at home. Although the money is tax-free in the country that you play in, and you will be credited for the amount of taxes that the Club team pays if you file there, you still have to declare it to the IRS here in the states. I found out the hard way. Initially, I was under the impression that I didn't have to pay taxes. By my 8th year in Europe, I was making substantial money and had acquired apartments, cars, etc. in the states. I was advised to start declaring my earnings to the IRS or that they could audit me and possibly take everything back. That summer, I did it. They asked when was the last time I had filed and how long I had been playing. To make a long story short, I was forced to pay for the previous 7 years of earnings along with late penalties and interest totaling over $100,000. Get a financial adviser, a tax guy, preferably someone who has dealt with Ex-patriots. You don't want to put yourself in a situation where you are paying interest and late fees for money that was already taxed. Do it right from the beginning because in the end, the IRS will always win."

# READY FOR YOUR JOURNEY?

HOPEFULLY THIS WILL HELP YOU GET STARTED ON THE RIGHT PATH TO A LONG AND PROSPEROUS CAREER. DON'T BE AFRAID TO TRAIL BLAZE. THERE ARE INFINITE AVENUES TO HAVING A GREAT BASKETBALL CAREER AROUND THE WORLD, TO WRITE YOUR OWN STORY. KEEP HEALTH AND FAMILY AS YOUR PRIORITIES AT ALL TIMES AND IT WILL PAY OFF FOR YOU. IF YOU MAKE YOUR DECISIONS WITH THESE THINGS IN MIND, YOU WILL FIND YOURSELF IN THE SITUATION THAT IS USUALLY THE BEST FOR YOUR FUTURE. THAT WAY, IF YOU MAKE A DECISION AND A DOOR OPENS FOR YOU IN THE BASKETBALL WORLD, YOU CAN RUN THROUGH IT WITH CONFIDENCE AND WITHOUT HESITATION. THERE IS NO ROOM FOR FEAR AND TENTATIVENESS IN THE WORLD OF SPORTS. AGGRESSIVENESS AND SMARTS PAY OFF, BOTH ON AND OFF THE COURT.

KEEP IN MIND THE KEYS WE HAVE REITERATED IN THE JOURNEYMAN'S GUIDE:

✓ **PREPARE LIKE A PRO!**

✓ **DO YOUR HOMEWORK, STAY INFORMED.**

✓ **KEEP YOUR REPUTATION INTACT.**

✓ **BE CONFIDENT AND PERFORM.**

## BEST OF LUCK IN YOUR CAREER!

# ABOUT THE AUTHORS

# RONALD BURRELL

Ronnie graduated from the University of North Carolina at Greensboro (UNCG) in 2005 with a degree in marketing, after receiving numerous accolades as an All-Southern Conference player and All-Conference academic honors. After working out for the former Charlotte Bobcats and Washington Wizards, Burrell went undrafted and moved to the Atlanta area to train with former college teammate James Maye while playing in a local minor league called the World Basketball Association. He changed agents over the summer before even signing his first deal overseas. That summer he signed his first deal in Europe to play in Levallois, France for a second division team just outside of Paris. After ranking among the top scorers in the league and earning a shot with the Seattle Supersonics (now OKC Thunder) to participate in mini-camp and summer league, Ronnie caught the attention of many European coaches.

In 2006 he signed with up and coming Serbian coach Sasa Obradovic and the reigning German champion, RheinEnergie Koln. Here, he learned how to play the European game on the highest level and participated in the Euroleague for the first time. He played alongside current NBA center Marcin Gortat to make up an athletic and formidable front line for a very good team that won the German Cup Championship. After playing with the Supersonics for a second summer, this time alongside top picks Kevin Durant and Jeff Green, Ronald's NBA dream never panned out. He opted for a second year in Germany with Telekom Bonn, where he led the team to the finals and made an All-Star game appearance. Burrell had developed a name for himself in the Bundesliga. However, he left the comfortable lifestyle of Germany to play in Poland and return to the Euroleague with Asseco Prokom.

For the next three years (2008-2011) Ronnie would enjoy his greatest success. Completing a three-peat of the Polish Championship while competing in the Euroleague and VTB league, made up of the top teams in Eastern Europe. In 2010, Burrell earned the reputation of a versatile frontcourt enforcer on, what is widely considered, the best Polish basketball team ever. They reached the quarterfinals of the Euroleague eventually losing a series to perennial contender Olympiacos Piraeus of Greece. However, Prokom had cemented its name in the top 10 teams in Europe that year. Burrell completed his Euroleague campaign at 55 games.

In 2011, Burrell went back to Germany and enjoyed four more years with two teams, EWE Oldenburg and Medi Bayreuth. Between 2011 and 2015 he would take another trip to the Bundesliga finals, participate in the FIBA Eurochallenge final four in Izmir, Turkey and be named Eurobasket All German League Honorable Mention in 2014.

In 2016, Burrell returned to France to finish his career where it began in 2005. He has retired from his playing career as of April 2016 and has joined the men's basketball staff at Florida Atlantic University. He has traveled to over twenty countries in Europe to compete during his career. Ronnie's career embodies the journey of a true professional that stuck with teams and leagues for long durations because of his reliability and toughness.

During off seasons, Ronald resides in the suburban Atlanta area with his wife Stefanie and daughter Camryn. Camryn was born November 5th, 2014 in Bamberg, Germany during his playing days with Medi Bayreuth. Ronald is an avid reader, boxing fan, and golfer.

BC Orchies/ Lille Metropole, France 2015-16
Medi Bayreuth, Germany 2013-15
*Eurobasket All Bundesliga Honorable Mention*
EWE Oldenburg, Germany 2011-13
*German Bundesliga Finalist*
*FIBA Eurochallenge Semifinalist*
Asseco Prokom, Poland 2008-11
*3X Polish Champion*
*Euroleague quarterfinalist*
*Eurobasket All Polish League Honorable Mention*
Telekom Bonn, Germany 2007-08
*German Bundesliga Finalist*
*Eurobasket All Bundesliga and All imports 1st Team*
RheinEnergie Koln, Germany 2006-07
*German Cup Champion*
*Euroleague week 4 MVP*
Levallois SCB, France 2005-06
Gainesville Knight, WBA 2005

# JAMES MAYE

After receiving numerous All-Southern Conference Awards, All-Conference Academic Honors and etching his name throughout his school's record books, James graduated from the University of North Carolina at Greensboro (UNCG) academically in 2002 with a Bachelor's Degree in Marketing. He finished his collegiate athletic career a year later in 2003, while completing his Post-Baccalaureate Certificate in Business Administration. Passing up a few opportunities waiting for a shot at the NBA dream, he began his career in Norway in late September after spending most of the summer training in Atlanta with former Memphis Grizzlies scout, Scott Adubato.

In 2004, his second professional season, he went full-blown into European play to hone his skills and knowledge of the game. He signed in the strong Greek League with ULEB cup team PAOK Thessaloniki, a team built with 8 national team members of various countries, finishing 4th in the Greek league and 5th in ULEB competition, losing in the elite 8. While in Greece, James took advantage of his free time, using it to attend the American College of Thessaloniki. He obtained his Masters of Business Administration with a specialty in Marketing by the end of the summer 2005.

He spent the next 2 years chasing the NBA dream, playing in the CBA and NBA D-League for the Dakota Wizards, whom eventually won the championship under now NBA head coach Dave Joerger. His tenure earned him various NBA mini-camp and summer league invites, and workouts with the Spurs, Nuggets, Raptors, Nets, Knicks, Hawks, and Lakers. Over these years, he mixed it up with perennial all stars of his position amongst many others of the elite, as well as gained a wealth of knowledge under Hall of Fame caliber coaches Phil Jackson and Gregg Popovich amongst others. James continued his European stint in countries such as France, Ukraine, and Poland. During those years, he also mixed in a championship season in Japan's top league, ventured to Libya to participate briefly for their country in international competition, included a stop in Iran where they lost in the Finals, as well as played in Australia.

In 2009, James began to cross over between European seasons by using the summers to translate his career into the Latin markets, introducing himself to Venezuela, Puerto Rico, Colombia, Mexico and Argentina. He made a big splash, putting up outstanding numbers, making him highly sought after. The biggest…in none other than Dominican Republic, where he obtained a passport after being nationalized and represented the Dominican Republic Men's National Team in international competition. His biggest stage came playing against the likes of Team USA in 2014 and NBA All Stars including former fellow SoCon player Steph Curry.

James has had a long successful career, still playing in his 14th season as of fall 2016. He has won 6 championships, 1 MVP and player of the year, 4 all-star appearances, and 1 all-star 3-point championship all while sustaining a 50/40/90 career average (50% from 2pt, 40% from 3pt, 90% from free throw line). Having touched 6 of 7 continents playing, he epitomizes to the fullest what being a Journeyman means.

During the offseason, James resides in the suburban Atlanta area with his wife Jasmin and daughter Aubrey. James is bilingual speaking English and Spanish. He is known to be a basketball junkie, passing his wealth of knowledge on to younger players on and off the court through training and guidance. He loves bowling, billiards, drawing and playing cards.

Dominican Republic National Team 2014-2016
*Bronze Medal Centrobasket '14*
*Top 5 scorer Pan-American Games Toronto '15*
Titanes del Distrito, Dominican Republic
2011-2016
*Team Captain, Numerous week MVP, 3-point record single game, 2x championship runner up*
BSN, Puerto Rico 2009-14, 16
*Mayaguez '09 '10, Humacao '11 '14, Guaynabo '12, Bayamon '13, Ponce '16*
*3x All-Star, 3-point champion, 2x top 5 scorer*
Eastern, Hong Kong 2015
*Championship, League MVP*
Argentina 2011-12,15
*Obras '11, Quilmes '11 '12, Ferrocarril Oeste 2015*
Toros de Maracay, Venezuela 2009, 13, 14
*Top 5 scorer*
Halcones Rojos de Veracruz, Mexico 2013
Zastal Zielona Gora, Poland 2010-11
Gold Coast Blaze, Australia 2010
Zob Ahan, Iran 2010
*Championship runner-up*
PBG Basket Poznan, Poland 2009-10
*All-Star*
Colombia 2009, 12
*Championship, League MVP*
Club Barias, Dominican Republic 2009
*Championship*
Al Shabob, Libya 2008
*Bronze Medal*
Aishin Sea Horses, Japan 2007-08
*League and Cup Championship, Top free throw percentage*
Khimik Yuzhny, Ukraine 2007
*League Bronze Medal*
Dakota Wizards, NBDL 2006-07
*Championship*
Paris Basket Racing, France 2006
Dakota Wizards, CBA 2005-06
PAOK Thessaloniki, Greece 2004-05
*Top 8 ULEB*
Rome Gladiators, WBA 2004
Marinos de Anzoategui, Venezuela 2004
Asker Aliens, Norway 2003-04
*League top scorer*

Made in the USA
San Bernardino, CA
23 February 2017